Y0-BVP-394

Dear Parents:

Children learn to read in stages, and all children develop reading skills at different ages. **Ready Readers**™ were created to promote children's interest in reading and to increase their reading skills. **Ready Readers**™ are written on two levels to accommodate children ranging in age from three through eight. These stages are meant to be used only as a guide.

Stage 1: Preschool-Grade 1
Stage 1 books are written in very short, simple sentences with large type. They are perfect for children who are getting ready to read or are just becoming familiar with reading on their own.

Stage 2: Grades 1-3
Stage 2 books have longer sentences and are a bit more complex. They are suitable for children who are able to read but still may need help.

All the **Ready Readers**™ tell varied, easy-to-follow stories and are colorfully illustrated. Reading will be fun, and soon your child will not only be ready, but eager to read.

Copyright © 1996 Modern Publishing
A Division of Unisystems, Inc.

™ Ready Readers is a trademark owned by Modern Publishing, a division of Unisystems, Inc. All rights reserved.

®Honey Bear Books is a trademark owned by Honey Bear Productions, Inc., and is registered in the U.S. Patent and Trademark Office.

All Rights Reserved.

No part of this book may be reproduced or copied in any format without written permission from the publisher.

Printed in the U.S.A.

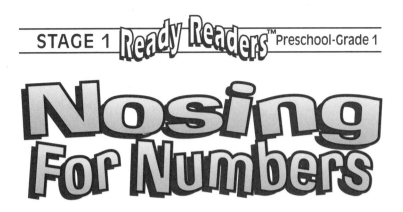

Nosing For Numbers

Written by M.C. Leeka
Illustrated by Florie Freshman

Modern Publishing
A Division of Unisystems, Inc.
New York, New York 10022

We're nosing for numbers.
We're on the right track.

We'll go to the toy store
And search every rack.

Nosing for numbers
Can be lots of fun.
First on our list is
To find number 1.

See the toy horns,
Toy pianos and drums!
Look carefully now –
For more number 1s.

There are dolls and a dollhouse,
All shiny and new.
If we look at them all,
Will we find number 2?

We'll follow our noses
And hope for a clue.
You never can tell
When you'll find the next 2.

Come look at the trains
And the airplanes that soar.
If we keep up our search,
We can find 3 and 4.

Now let's try the aisle
Where they keep pogo sticks.

Keep your eyes open
To find 5 and 6.

Here are the wagons
And scooters and skates.
Do you think we'll spot
Any 7s or 8s?

You look in the saucers,
I'll look in the plates.
That way we won't miss
Any 7s or 8s.

See the toy soldiers,
All standing in line.
Maybe they know
Where to find number 9.

There may be some numbers
Near Jack-in-the-box.
Perhaps 8 or 9 is near
Puppets or blocks.

Let's study the cars,
And the fire engine truck.
We might find a 10,
If we have any luck.

We thank you for helping us
Find 1 through 10.
We hope to go nosing
For numbers again.

Did you
find all the
hidden
numbers?

Ready Readers™ are the perfect books to help the beginning reader get started on a lifetime of reading fun.

This is a Stage 1 book, written especially for children who are getting ready to read or are beginning to read on their own.

Nosing For Numbers

Young readers will delight in searching out numbers hidden in each charming picture. The lively rhyming text contains clever clues.

Titles in this Series

Modern Publishing
A Division of Unisystems, Inc.
New York, New York 10022
Printed in the U.S.A.

ISBN 1-56144-946-6

0 30099 29580